Children of the World

India

For their help in the preparation of *Children of the World: India*, the editors gratefully thank Employment and Immigration Canada, Ottawa, Ont.; the US Immigration and Naturalization Service, Washington, DC; the United States Department of State, Bureau of Public Affairs, Office of Public Communication, Washington, DC, for unencumbered use of material in the public domain; and Pratul Pathak, Milwaukee.

Library of Congress Cataloging-in-Publication Data

India.

(Children of the world)
Bibliography: p.
Includes index.
Summary: Presents the life of a young Indian boy from Jodhpur, Rajasthan, describing his school, home, family, amusements, and some of the customs and celebrations of his country.
1. India—Juvenile literature. 2. Children—India—Juvenile literature. [1. Family life—India. 2. India—Social life and customs] I. Uchiyama, Sumio. II. Knowlton, MaryLee. III. Wright, David K. IV. Series: Children of the world (Milwaukee, Wis.)
DS407.I445   1988   954   87-42577
ISBN 1-55532-233-6
ISBN 1-55532-208-5 (lib. bdg.)

North American edition first published in 1988 by

Gareth Stevens, Inc.
7317 West Green Tree Road
Milwaukee, Wisconsin 53223, USA

This work was originally published in shortened form consisting of section I only. Photographs and original text copyright © 1986 by Uchiyama Sumio. First and originally published by Kaisei-sha Publishing Co., Ltd., Tokyo. World English rights arranged with Kaisei-sha Publishing Co., Ltd. through Japan Foreign-Rights Centre.

Copyright this format © 1988 by Gareth Stevens, Inc.
Additional material and maps copyright © 1988 by Gareth Stevens, Inc.

Typeset by Ries Graphics ltd., Milwaukee.
Design: Laurie Bishop.
Map design: Sheri Gibbs.

1 2 3 4 5 6 7 8 9 93 92 91 90 89 88

Children of the World
India

Photography by
Uchiyama Sumio

Edited by
MaryLee Knowlton
David K. Wright

Gareth Stevens Publishing
Milwaukee

. . . a note about *Children of the World:*

The children of the world live in fishing towns, Arctic regions, and urban centers, on islands and in mountain valleys, on sheep ranches and fruit farms. This series follows one child in each country through the pattern of his or her life. Candid photographs show the children with their families, at school, at play, and in their communities. The text describes the dreams of the children and, often through their own words, tells how they see themselves and their lives.

Each book also explores events that are unique to the country in which the child lives, including festivals, religious ceremonies, and national holidays. The *Children of the World* series does more than tell about foreign countries. It introduces the children of each country and shows readers what it is like to be a child in that country.

. . . and about *India:*

Vikram Singh, whose nickname is Viku, is from Jodhpur, Rajasthan. He is in his first year of boarding school. Viku's father, grandfather, and great-grandfather all work or once worked for the Maharaja of Jodhpur. Viku's ambition is to be a soldier when he grows up.

To enhance this book's value in libraries and classrooms, comprehensive reference sections include up-to-date data about India's geography, demographics, currency, education, culture, industry, and natural resources. *India* also features a bibliography, research topics, activity projects, and discussions of such subjects as New Delhi, the country's history, political system, ethnic and religious composition, and language.

The living conditions and experiences of children in India vary tremendously according to economic, environmental, and ethnic circumstances. The reference sections help bring to life for young readers the diversity and richness of the culture and heritage of India. Of particular interest are discussions of the vast historical background of India and of the tremendous role played by India as both active participant and awkward mediator in the ethnic and political tumult of its region.

CONTENTS

Viku's family from left, his mother, Chanda; father, Sunder; sister Kavita; Viku; and his sister Sweety. The dog's name is Tommy.

LIVING IN INDIA:
Viku, a Child of Wealth

Meet Vikram Singh, known to his friends and family as Viku. Viku lives in the city of Jodhpur in India with his father, Sunder Singh; his mother, Chanda; his older sisters, Kavita and Sweety; and his grandmother. The dog, Tommy, is a member of the family, too.

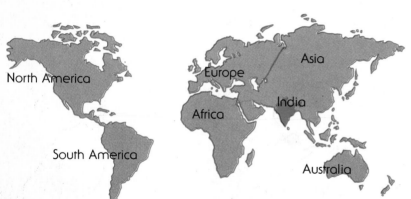

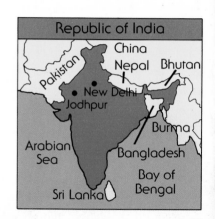

Vikram Singh and his father.

The city of Jodhpur.

Viku's father is the secretary of Gaj Singh, the Maharaja of Jodhpur. His family has worked for the Maharajas for generations. Sunder Singh manages the palace and fields of the Maharaja, schedules his appointments with visitors from other parts of India and abroad, and takes notes at meetings.

In the past India had about 100 Maharajas who ruled as kings. Since 1947 they are no longer kings with power to rule. They have the same rights as any other citizen but retain their great wealth. The Maharaja of Jodhpur is still an important person to the people, who respect his kindness and look to him for advice and assistance.

The Maharaja and his family.

The palace at night.

People say, "Kamigari," when they greet a member of the Jodhpur royal family. They join their hands in front of their chest and bow slightly from the waist.

Viku and Shivraj, the son of the Maharaja, are great friends. When Viku was younger, his father heard him bragging of this friendship. He told Viku that he should take pride in what he does, not who his friends are.

Jodhpur is in the state of Rajasthan, where most of the people belong to the warrior caste called Rajput. In the 16th century, when the king of the Moghul Empire attacked, the Rajputs fought back so bravely that they were said to be like lions. The name Singh means lion and all descendants of the Rajputs — the Maharaja, the peasants, and Viku, too — have the same last name.

Viku and his friend Shivraj, dressed in formal clothing.

Viku greets the Maharaja.

11

The living room of Viku's house is arranged to catch the fresh breezes.

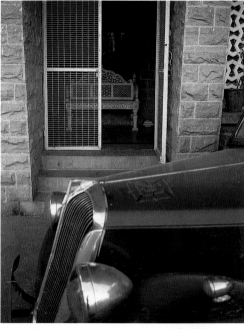

An antique car awaits parts from England.

Three servants keep the household running smoothly.

Viku's house is large and comfortable. It is made of stone, with many doors and windows to keep the air flowing freely. His family has three male servants who work inside the house.

Outside the house sits an old car that belonged to Viku's grandfather. It hasn't gone anywhere in years. Viku's father plans to get parts from England to repair the car.

Sunder Singh's work for the Maharaja keeps him away from home much of the time. Viku's mother, Chanda, is in charge of the children and the servants.

Like most married Indian women, Chanda Singh wears a *saree*. Indian sculptures and murals over 5,000 years old show women draped in the saree, a piece of cloth 6-9 yards (5-8 meters) long. The saree can be either cotton or silk and is embroidered or dyed in an endless variety of designs. You can sometimes tell what part of the country a woman is from by the way she drapes her saree. Most often it is pleated and draped over one shoulder. Chanda Singh wears hers draped like a full length gown.

Viku and his mother, in Indian clothing. Chanda Singh wears a saree and a tika.

Viku's mother also wears the red spot on her forehead known as a *tika* or *bindi*. In legend it was known as the third eye, a source of strength and wisdom. Today it usually means the woman is married.

Indian men of Viku's class are likely to dress like men from Europe or America in suits and ties. When they dress in Indian clothing, they wear a dress coat called a *sherwani* and tight pants called *churidor.*

The whole family together for lunch — a special time!

Today the whole family is together for lunch, an unusual occasion. Breakfast is a light meal of tea and fruit. But lunch and dinner are large and varied, with dishes prepared by Viku's mother and sisters. They have *chapati*, which is Indian bread, a lentil dish called *daal*, vegetables, yogurt, and curry made with chicken or lamb. Curry is seasoned with a blend of spices called a *masaala*. Each family makes its own blend from saffron, coriander, chili pepper, black pepper, cardamom, and laurel. The flavor of the masaala depends on the amount of each spice.

Lunch: Meat and vegetable curries and chapati.

Viku eats gracefully with his right hand.

Sometimes the family eats with knives and forks, but more often they tear off pieces of chapati and scoop and roll the other food in it. Viku can eat both ways and follows the example of his elders when he's not sure which to use.

In the yard Viku takes care of a calf that has lost its mother.

The Traditions of Viku's Life

Children of Viku's social class do not play in rowdy ways or get themselves dirty. From the time they are little, they are taught by their parents to play at things that will be useful to them in the future. Viku takes this for granted.

Viku plays mostly in his own yard. He cuts the grass with a friend or practices hunting with his father's gun and his dog. Hunting is regulated in India. You can't hunt tigers, for instance. Gun possession is tightly controlled, and it is very hard to get a gun permit.

The traditions of India have as much to do with how people live as the laws do. When laws and traditions are in conflict, most people will follow their traditions. For example, the caste system has been illegal for 40 years in India. According to the caste system, people were born into one of four groups, or castes, and had rights and duties as a result of their birth. Today, legally, all people have the same rights, but most people order their lives according to the old ways anyway.

Viku is allowed to use his father's gun.

Cutting the grass is fun with a friend.

The caste system comes from the Hindu religion, the world's oldest living religion. The castes take their names from the parts of the body of Prajapati, the lord of all creatures. The Brahma caste comes from the head, and its role is to study and teach. It is the highest caste. The second, the Kashatriya, is the caste from which Viku's family comes. It is the caste of warriors and rulers. The Vaishya is the merchant caste. The fourth caste is the Shudra, the servant caste. Below these four castes are the Untouchables, sometimes called the fifth caste. Their lot in life is to do the most menial work.

The family has a refreshment stand in the yard for guests.

Viku looks for Tommy. The yard has many hiding places for a little dog.

Viku's sisters can all read and write. Being from a wealthy family makes a big difference in a woman's life in India.

The government has programs to improve the lives of women in India — programs to provide health care, to teach adult women to read, to teach job skills, to provide nutrition education for women with children. An equal rights law makes it illegal to deny a woman a job or to pay her less than a man.

These policies and programs have only begun to have effects in India. Most women have few rights or opportunities. Over 75% of them still cannot read.

Viku is proud of the small hut he has made from straw and mud.

India is a land of many religions, but 80% of the people are Hindu. Vikram's is a family of devout believers. At six each morning, they awake, take a shower to purify themselves, wash their faces, brush their teeth, and go to the temple in the garden for *puja*, which means prayer. They cannot enter the temple wearing leather, so they leave their shoes at the entrance.

Today, when they return to the house after puja, they find Ruby, Vikram's oldest sister, waiting. She lives nearby with her husband and baby boy. In India, particularly in this region, it is considered good to marry young and have many children.

India has a problem because its population is greater than the country's economy can support and feed. The government has many programs for slowing the growth of the population. As in many other areas of their lives, however, Indians look to tradition in making decisions. As a result, many families still have many children, and boys are especially desirable.

Morning puja in the garden temple.

A visit from Viku's sister Ruby and her baby.

There is a military base in Jodhpur, because it is close to India's border with Pakistan. India and Pakistan are not on good terms, and from early morning jet fighter planes take off, engines roaring, on reconnaissance missions near the border. Viku does not know much about war, but he does know that when he grows up he wants to defend his country and the people who are important to him.

The father of his friend Channi is an Air Force captain. He is being transferred to a base in the state of Assam. Channi will be leaving in a month. The boys are saddened by the thought of being separated. They have played and studied together since they were very small boys. They make plans to get together. Viku thinks that, if he studies hard, his father will take him to Assam by plane.

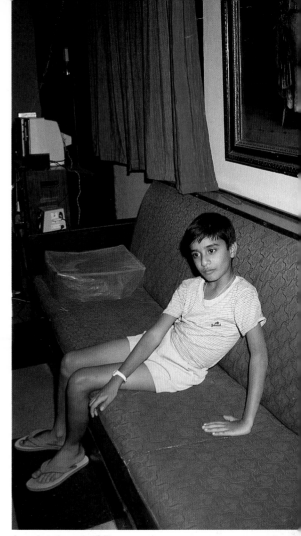

A quiet time for Viku.

Viku's friend Channi helps Viku with his vacation homework. Viku is preparing for the school year.

21

The Market

Viku loves to go into Jodhpur shopping with his mother. Here, cows wander up and down the street, even though Jodhpur is a city of 300,000 people. When a cow can no longer give milk, its owner abandons it, and it is left to wander around freely. Hindus believe that cows are messengers of God, so people give leftover vegetables or other food to stray cows, and they do not eat beef.

The marketplace is always crowded, but not with cars. In India only about one person in 100 owns a car. About twice that many have motorcycles. Most people walk or ride bikes. Some come to the market by bus from other parts of the city.

Cattle are the messengers of God. People feed them and treat them with respect.

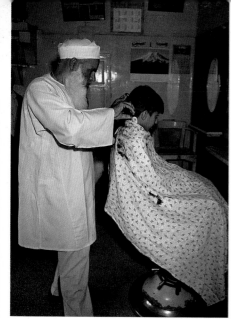
Viku gets a haircut. His barber is a Muslim.

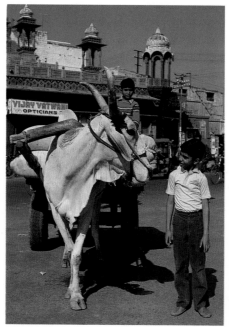
A ride in a cattle cart.

The market is the best place for fresh vegetables.

The market in Jodhpur is a wonderful place. Although there are small shops near Viku's house, things at the market are fresher and cheaper. Viku's mother does most of her shopping here.

The market grew up under the castle. It is a maze of little streets that are very confusing till you see the order there. Each street has a certain kind of shop — one street for vegetables, one for fabric, one for candy, whatever you want.

◄ The marketplace spreads out beneath the old fort of Jodhpur.

Shops in the marketplace — a shop for everything.

The shopping is done by women.

Houses in the city. The palace is in the background.

When Chanda Singh finishes her shopping, she and Viku do his shopping. She knows just what he wants. Every shopping day they make the same rounds.

First they go to the candy store for the nuts and chocolate that Viku loves. Next comes the toy store. He can't find any new models of the toy cars he collects, so his mother buys him a toy gun instead.

The last stop is the bookstore. Viku looks at the rows and rows of movie magazines to find one for his sister. India produces more movies than any other country in the world. Every major city has at least 100 theaters. Viku finds a magazine Kavita will like. It features Amitab, an actor who always plays a defender of justice. Amitab is a national hero to Indians, both children and adults. Other actors and actresses are also highly respected.

It's hard to pick out just one kind of candy.

It's even harder to find just the right magazine.

A toy shop.

27

Students line up for meals.

The dormitories at Mayo College — Viku's other home.

New School Life

Till this year, Viku has gone to school in Jodphur and lived
at home. This year he will attend boarding school 200 miles
(320 km) from home in Ajmer. The caste system in India has
traditionally meant that people associated only with members
of their own caste. So, many years ago, Maharajas built Mayo
College for the education of their sons. Today, the school is open
to non-royal children, too. It even has students from outside India,
mostly from the Middle East. Though it's called a college, the
school is really like an American prep school, with grades from
5th grade through high school.

Viku's class. Mayo College has five first year classes.

Viku's friend Shivraj, the son of the Maharaja, also goes to school
here. Viku will be attending Mayo College for the next eight years.
The school is divided into two groups, the junior and senior classes.
Viku is in the first year of the junior class.

The boys study Hindi, India's national language, and English,
math, science, social studies, art, and physical education.
Educational standards are very high, because these students
are from wealthy families, and many will go on to college in
foreign countries. The teachers are kind, but they are also strict.
The children must grow up quickly away from home. One day,
the physical education teacher shook his fist at Viku in anger,
but Viku didn't flinch.

Social studies class: Classes meet six days a week.

Viku's teachers.

Viku has six classes a day. Each one lasts for an hour. There is a ten-minute break between classes and an hour for lunch. His favorite class is English, because the teacher loves the plays of Shakespeare and has taught her students to love them, too.

After they've studied a play for a while, the students take parts and act out scenes from the play. Viku once played Romeo in a scene from *Romeo and Juliet.*

The students have all their meals in the cafeteria. Breakfast is tea, toast, and eggs. Lunch and dinner are Indian foods, chapati and curry, just like at home.

Hindi class: Viku practices his reading and pronunciation.

Viku and Shivraj eat lunch together and make plans to play after classes.

The junior class art exhibit.

All the students at Mayo College live in dormitories. Junior students can only leave campus with their families or with a senior classman. Each dormitory room has 40 boys in it. Viku and Shivraj are in the same room, though they are in different classes. Each boy has a locker for his uniforms, other clothes, sports equipment, and treasures. Dirty clothes go into a laundry bag. Every Tuesday morning, a man picks up the bags of dirty laundry. In the evening he returns the clothes, all clean.

The boys gladly change clothes before sports practice.

A letter from home. Viku reads it over and over.

Viku's locker.

Each dorm room has 40 beds.

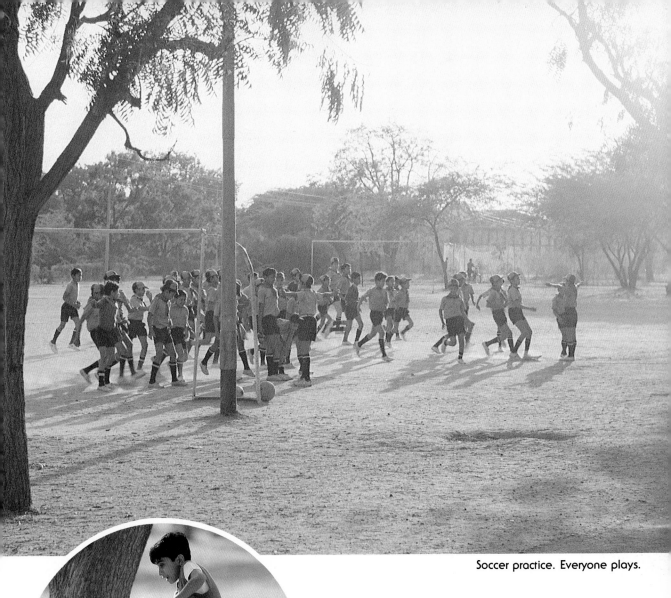

Soccer practice. Everyone plays.

Viku practices his cricket.
He wants to get really good.

Today Viku gets a letter from home, and he and Shivraj read it carefully. Then, before they can feel too homesick, a friend comes to get them for cricket, and they run off to play. With dinner at seven-thirty and lights out at nine, the boys don't have much free time. Viku uses every chance he gets to play cricket.

33

A Land of Festivals

The most beautiful of Indian festivals is Diwali, which honors Lakshmi, the goddess of wealth. On Diwali night, the night of November's new moon, the people light their porches and entrances with oil lamps.

Playing with firecrackers.

To celebrate, the Maharaja throws a big party at the palace. While His Highness and Viku's father talk with the guests, Viku and the other children light firecrackers. The huge palace gardens are filled with the pops of firecrackers and the laughter of children.

Holi is the most lively of the Hindu festivals. It is celebrated all over the north of India as the beginning of spring. Men, women, and children throw colored powder and squirt colored water at each other.

Vendors sell colored powder for the Holi festival.

People celebrate Holi by sprinkling red powder and water on each other.

Jodhpur at night. The palace is lighted up for the celebration.

A desert fire warms the campers. The night is cold.

Two camels, mother and baby.

The campers are a large party: Viku's family, the Maharaja's family, and many servants.

Camping In the Desert

Every year at the end of December, just before Viku returns to school, the family goes camping for a week. They stay in the desert near the town of Pokharan, 125 miles (200 km) from Jodhpur. This year the Maharaja's family has come along. Viku loves having his friend Shivraj to play with. The families bring vegetables and meat for cooking and build a campfire in the desert. They are surrounded by nothing but wild animals and birds. Camping out in the wild is a treat for these two worldly urban families.

Viku and Shivraj help carry the milk.

Horseback riding practice. A boy of Viku's class must ride well.

राजकीय प्राथमिक विद्यालय ॐ गुड़ा खुर्द प॰ स॰ लूनि

School in a Desert Village

About 10 miles (16 km) from Jodhpur, in a desert area, is the village of Gurukul. A few years ago, a wealthy man from Jodhpur built a small school there for the people of the village. Here Mr. Babban teaches 21 children from grades one to five. Only two of the students are girls.

Kiran works on his Hindi pronunciation.

The students write on slates.

The school has just a few books.

Classes meet outdoors.

The school at Gurukul. The students and their teacher are like a family. Many students are from other villages far away.

The students play games during physical education class.

It rarely rains in Gurukul, so classes are usually held outdoors in the shade. The children study reading and writing Hindi, social studies, science, math, and physical education. The school has some textbooks, but the children don't use notebooks. They write on slates with a soft stone that can be erased.

Mr. Babban writes lessons for each class on blackboards. He spends 15 minutes with each group of children. The 1st graders are learning to write the names of plants and animals. The 2nd graders are learning to add and subtract. The 3rd graders are studying science. Mr. Babban is kept very busy working at all these different levels. These children are very lucky. Only 36% of the people of India can read, and not many of them are poor children like these.

Kiran and his uncle's family: Children from other villages are part of the family, too.

Ready for school.

An eight-year-old boy, Kiran, lives in Gurukul. Three years ago, when the school was built, his parents sent him there to live with his uncle and aunt. Kiran's parents and four younger brothers live in a village far away. The family is very poor and its village does not have a school. Three other boys from other villages live with Kiran's aunt and uncle, too. They are really not lonesome, because they have formed their own kind of family.

Getting water from the well.

Kiran goes home for lunch.

The house of Kiran's uncle.

Kiran's school is right behind his house, less than a minute away. Before and after school the boys help the villagers. One hundred people live in this village with just one well. Drawing water in the morning and evening is the women's work, but the children must help. Even little children come to the well with water pots on their heads. Kiran and the other boys fill the water pots and put them on the children's heads.

Kiran's aunt making chapati.

India — The Children of Mohandas Gandhi

The people of India have a rich past. Their beliefs and customs differ from one region to another. Throughout history, these varied people have lived together in peace and acceptance of each other. However, for many years, they were not free. In this century, they were finally united under the loving and wise leadership of Mohandas K. Gandhi.

Bodh Gaya: Sister and brother.

"We have something more important than guns. We have truth and justice — and time — on our side. You cannot hold down much longer three hundred and fifty million people who are determined to be free." This was Mohandas K. Gandhi speaking, telling the British that India would someday be free of British rule. He was right.

South India: Trivandrun fisherpeople.

A baby's cradle.

With Gandhi's belief in *satyagraha,* he led his people to freedom. Satyagraha is a method of non-violent civil disobedience. It was and still is a simple method. Before Gandhi, people knew only violence as a method of fighting oppression. Gandhi taught his people to make fair demands, refuse to obey unjust laws, and, most importantly, not fight back when they were attacked. Today, all over the world, we see peaceful protest demonstrations and boycotts as a natural way of fighting wrongs.

South India: Cochin elephant handler.

People from Ladakh, the northernmost part of India.

Bathing in the Ganges River.

South India: Tea vendor.

Pushkar fair, a desert livestock market.

A child of Kashmir.

Village women carrying water.

In the United States, the Rev. Martin Luther King led people in marches to racially integrate schools and public places, and to allow people of all races to vote and to live where they chose. Today, throughout the world, people allow themselves to be arrested and jailed in protests against the spread of nuclear weapons.

Gandhi's method, though peaceful, does not guarantee safety for its followers. The British were often merciless in their attacks on protesting Indians. Many died, and both Gandhi and Rev. King were murdered by people opposed to their values. Yet Gandhi urged his followers to accept the value of all life as a basis for their lives. "I hold myself to be incapable of hating any being on earth," he said.

A desert musician.

A village school in Ladakh.

The people of India call Gandhi the father of their country. The example he set for his followers was one of faith, wisdom, and action — the cornerstone of Hindu belief. He lived a simple life, free of material things.

Gandhi also urged the people of India to give up the cruelties built into the caste system. The caste system allowed those in higher castes to oppress or ignore the needs of people in the lower castes. In particular, the group outside the caste system known as the Untouchables was neglected and rejected. Gandhi fasted and protested on their behalf. His belief in the value of all life is part of the legacy he left India and the world.

A field of mustard.

FOR YOUR INFORMATION: India

Official Name: Bharat
(bah-RAHT)
Republic of India

Capital: New Delhi

History

The Dravidians, the Aryan Invaders, Alexander, and the Moghuls

India is the European name for the country that Indians call *Bharat*. The word comes from the Indus River valley in the far northwest. A modern society lived there, long before there were many towns in Europe. The first invaders were Aryans. They were wanderers from central Asia who overran the country in about 1500 BC. The Aryans were tall and light skinned. The people already living in India were Dravidians. They were shorter and darker. The Aryans spread the Hindu religion. They learned how to be a part of a complex society. To this day, the two main kinds of language come from the Aryans and Dravidians.

This building is typical of Moghul architecture of the 18th century.

Later invaders included Alexander the Great from southern Europe in 327 BC and Muslims from the Moghul empire of Persia in AD 1526. The Moghuls followed earlier Muslims, who had brought the religion of Islam to the country. The Moghuls were wonderful artists, architects, and rulers. The British arrived in 1612 to find a well-run country with beautiful buildings and strange and colorful art. The most famous example of Moghul design is the Taj Mahal. It is a temple built to honor one ruler's favorite wife. Some experts believe it is the most beautiful building on Earth.

India Under the British

The first British in India were members of the East India Trading Company. They built outposts in the large cities and made a lot of money buying spices, cloth, and other items they shipped to Europe and sold. The British government helped the trading company gain control of India by beating the French and the Moghuls in large battles. Between 1818 and 1849, the company became the rulers of India.

The British were fascinated by India but did not treat the people well. In 1857, Indian soldiers under British officers rebelled. For 14 months, the Indian Mutiny raged across the country, with thousands of men, women, and children killed on both sides. Because of the rebellion, the East India Company gave control of India to the British government.

During the 90 years of British control that followed, the wonder of India came to be known all over the world. A few British government officials ruled huge Indian states. But they allowed friendly maharajahs to run some of the states. English businessmen, journalists, and adventurers traveled all over the country. The stories they brought back to England made India seem the most desirable place in the British Empire.

But native Indians continued to suffer. Because they had little or no money, they were forced to perform work that was beneath their abilities. Old-time photos of Englishmen in India show Indian adults holding umbrellas, waving fans, or doing some other lowly task. Meanwhile, some Indians were being well educated. They went to famous English schools and colleges and returned to help run the country. These educated Indians, along with retired British officials, began the Indian National Congress political party in 1885. The party started as an organization to look after the interests of Indians who had an education. But it became the loudest voice in their cry for independence.

Gandhi and the Way to Independence

In 1914, an English-educated Indian named Mohandas K. Gandhi returned to India after living for 21 years in South Africa. The racial discrimination he had seen in Africa made him aware of the discrimination in his native land. Later he expressed his discovery this way: "I discovered that as a man and an Indian I had no rights. More correctly, I discovered that I had no rights as a man because I was an Indian."

Many other Indians felt the same way. They had only the rights the British gave them, and these were few and could easily be taken away. In 1919, there were huge demonstrations. The British fired into a crowd of unarmed Indians in the city of Amritsar. They killed almost 400 innocent people. This massacre helped unify the people and gave strength to the Independence Movement.

Gandhi became head of the Indian National Congress in 1920. Gandhi taught his followers the principle of *satyagraha*, a word which refers to the power of truth to force change. Following Gandhi's method, people refused to cooperate with the British authorities when they felt the laws were unjust. They accepted the consequences of their decisions. Even when they were beaten or jailed, they did not resort to violence. Satyagraha is sometimes called a peaceful or passive resistance. It is not passive, however. It is very active, but it excludes violence on the part of the resisters. It is only peaceful if the resisters are not attacked despite their non-violent ways. In India the British often responded to satyagraha with violence.

The anti-British movement caused the government big problems in World War II. As the Japanese army moved toward India, the British did not know if they could trust Indian soldiers. Though it was non-violent, the movement was having an effect. Many Indians were jailed because they wanted to rule their own land.

India's Difficult Independence

Indians won their freedom in 1947. The first prime minister was Jawaharlal Nehru. Millions of Muslims who feared the Hindus fled to Pakistan. And likewise, millions of Hindus left Pakistan for India. Hundreds of thousands of these homeless people were murdered in riots throughout India. To make matters worse, Gandhi was shot to death because he continued to preach non-violence.

The country's huge population — 800 million people today — suffered greatly at first. There never seemed to be enough food, and disasters such as floods and droughts killed thousands. Nehru proclaimed his country neutral and received aid from many other nations. His success helped his daughter become the new prime minister in 1966.

Her name was Indira Gandhi. She was not related to Mohandas Gandhi. She had been educated in England and knew politics as well as her father when she took power. Other political parties were springing up to oppose the Congress party. They believed Mrs. Gandhi cheated in an election and they convinced a judge that she had done so. Mrs. Gandhi replied in 1975 by throwing many of her opponents in jail and taking away human rights. She was criticized around the world for this action but said the nation would not survive without such strong moves. The Supreme Court of India cleared her of any wrongdoing in the election.

Mrs. Gandhi lost an election in 1977, then returned to win an election in 1980.

She was shot to death by two members of the Sikh religion in 1984. They killed the prime minister because she had put down a rebellion among Sikhs in northern India. Her son, Rajiv Gandhi, succeeded her as prime minister.

India today is still a very complicated place. Oxen pull wooden plows in the shadow of a nuclear reactor. People live in cardboard boxes or in the street not far from luxury apartment buildings. Some Indians wish their country were still under British rule, while others belong to a communist party. Even with all of its many contradictions, in 40 years of independence India has made great progress.

Currency

The main units of Indian currency are the paise and the rupee. One hundred paises equal one rupee.

Government

India is a federal republic with a parliamentary type of government. The president is elected every five years. He or she is advised by the most powerful person in the country, who is the prime minister. The prime minister is the head of the largest political party. He or she is assisted by a cabinet of ministers.

The parliament has two houses, just as the British have a House of Lords and a House of Commons. In India, the two houses are the Council of States and the House of the People. The members of the Council of States are elected by state assemblies. Every adult can vote for the House of the People members. At least five different political parties are represented in parliament. Two are communist. Despite political differences, a coalition of small parties was formed to oppose the late prime minister, Indira Gandhi. It was successful in removing her from office but was divided in later elections and has since disbanded.

On a daily basis, India's government is large and slow. It serves an enormous population, of whom only about one-third can read. Procedures are complicated, and the amount of red tape involved in even the most minor action is discouraging to many Indians.

The country's foreign policy is not always successful. India says it is a nonaligned or neutral country, which means it does not take sides in international disputes. This does not mean, however, that it does not engage in disputes of its own. Since independence, India has had wars and disagreements with most of its neighbors. Areas that border Pakistan and China are scenes of continuing disputes. In the south, India's island neighbor, Sri Lanka, faces a civil war. A large Indian minority there has caused death and destruction. India has for several years traded heavily with the USSR, Japan, Saudi Arabia, and the US.

In the years immediately before and after independence, India was a leader of Third World countries. These were formerly backward nations that were developing modern industries and governments. India's leaders sent political and philosophical messages from the world's newest democracy. Today India is no longer a leader in the Third World. Its mammoth size and the complexity of its problems have set it apart from other countries and reduced its influence. Today, as always, the distance between the rich and the numberless poor is great. In parts of India political violence and government repression occur, though not as often as outsiders might expect. The promise that democracy holds makes many poor Indians feel that they have a voice which will be heard.

Religion

Hinduism

More than 80 percent of Indians are Hindus. The Hindu religion has no founder and allows followers to believe in no god, one god, or many. It features gods with blue skin, gods with elephant heads, and gods with a dozen arms. Hindus pick one of the millions of Hindu gods and worship him or her in temples and in front of altars in the home.

As the world's oldest major religion, Hinduism maintains that all religions and all gods are just different parts of the universal soul, or *Bramha*. Each human, animal, and plant is part of an endless series of being born, living, and dying. This is called reincarnation. The goal of Hindus is to break this endless chain by living a good life. They then become part of Bramha.

Especially important is the idea of caste. Everyone is born into a certain caste or place in society. High levels are priests, landowners, and warriors. Low levels include persons who sweep the streets or butcher animals. Low caste members must not do anything that will upset higher members. They must live a good life, even if the life they were born into is lowly. All Hindus must avoid any kind of

Worshippers at a shrine: Mysore Nandi Hills.

pollution. Pollution can happen if a Hindu accidentally eats beef, comes too close to a low-caste person, or fails to perform a religious ceremony correctly. Some Indians have rejected the caste system, which was banned soon after independence. They believe that much of the caste system is related to skin color and is therefore a sign of prejudice.

Buddhism

Several other religions began in India. The most important is Buddhism. Buddha was a prince who found enlightenment by leaving his palace and walking across northern India in 600 BC. Buddhism has only a few million followers in India, but it is the major religion of China and much of Southeast Asia.

Sikhism and Jainism

Sikhism and Jainism began in India. Sikhism is an attempt to bring together the best of Hinduism and Islam. Enmity between Sikhs and Hindus has caused serious violence in India in the past and it continues today. The Jains do not believe in the caste system and are forbidden to kill anything, even the smallest insect. India has about eight million Sikhs and 3.5 million Jains.

Islam

Muslims, people who follow the teachings of Mohammed, are members of the Islam religion. They number almost 80 million. Most Muslims live in the northern half of the country. They and the Sikhs are famed as soldiers, while the Jains include many holy men and many wealthy businessmen. There are dozens of other religions spread among primitive villages in central and south India.

Land

India is a subcontinent. That means it is almost as large as a continent. It also means that the land and the weather are very different from one place to another. The very northern parts of India have snowy, windy weather atop the world's tallest mountains. South of that is a vast plain, and below that is a huge plateau. The far south is usually warm, wet, and green.

The country is wide in the north and narrows to a point in the south. The southern half sticks into the Indian Ocean. The northern half has these Asian neighbors: Pakistan (to the west), China (north), and Nepal, Bangladesh, and Burma (east).

India is large. It measures over 1,800 miles (about 3,000 km) from east to west and 1,800 miles from north to south. The total area is 1,229,737 square miles (3,185,019 sq km). That is about one-third the size of the US. Besides the northern peaks, there are mountains along the east and west coasts and across the lower middle part of India. The mountains play a big part in India's varied climate.

INDIA — Political and Physical

GENERAL REFERENCE

Countries
INDIA

Regions
RAJASTHAN

New Delhi ■ Towns over 1,000,000
Patna ● Towns over 100,000
Thimphu ○ Towns under 100,000

▪▪▪ International Boundaries
Major Transportation Routes
Rivers
Regional Boundaries

Crops, Industry, and Natural Resources

Coal	Railroad Equipment	
Cotton	Rice	
Fish	Root Crops	
Fruit	Steel	
Mining	Tea	
Oil	Wood	

Vegetation/Products

Vegetation
Forest & Woodland
Grassland & Pasture
Nonagricultural & Desert

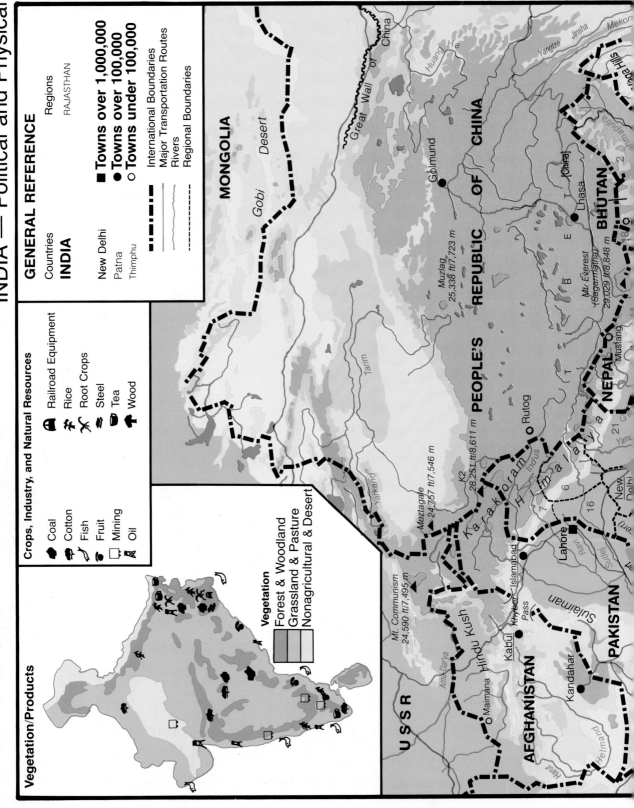

MONGOLIA

Gobi Desert

Great Wall of China

Huang He

Golmund

PEOPLE'S REPUBLIC OF CHINA

Muzlag, 25,338 ft/7,723 m

Tarim

Yarkand

Muztagale 24,757 ft/7,546 m

K2 28,251 ft/8,611 m

Karakoram

Indus

Himalaya

Rutog

Lhasa

BHUTAN

Mt. Everest (Sagarmatha) 29,029 ft/8,848 m

Mustang

NEPAL

Yamu

Mt. Communism 24,590 ft/7,495 m

Hindu Kush

Amu Darya

Maimana

Kabul

Khyber Pass

Islamabad

Sulaiman

Kandahar

Lahore

Ravi

Sutlej

PAKISTAN

AFGHANISTAN

U S S R

Helmand

Kabul

Jinsha

Yangtze

Mekong

China

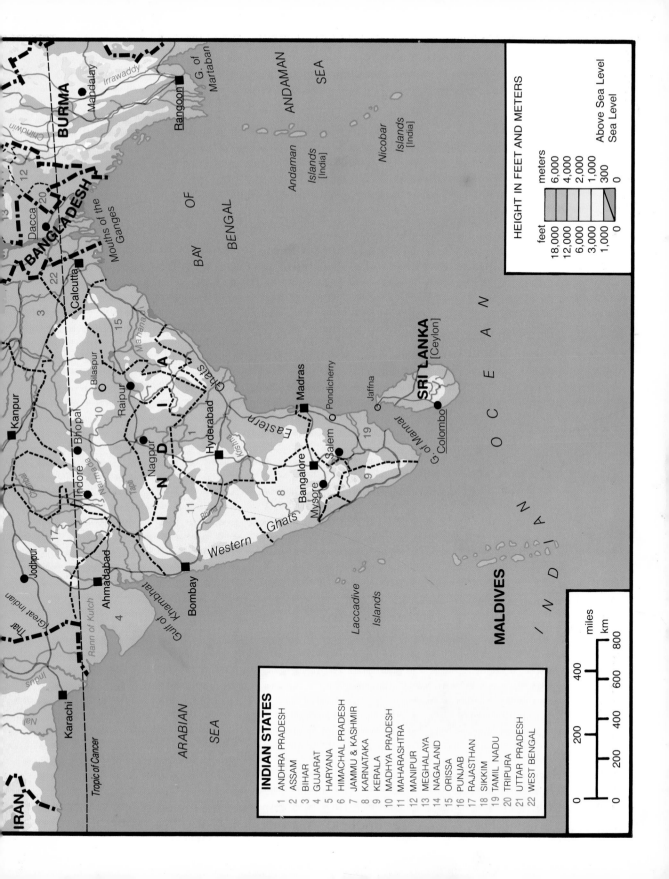

IRAN

BURMA

Mandalay

Irrawaddy

Chindwin

Chindwin

BANGLADESH

Dacca

13

12

20

22

3

DACCA

Mouths of the
Ganges

Calcutta

Mahanadi

15

Bilaspur

Raipur

10

I N D I A

Eastern Ghats

Nagpur

Narmada

1

Bhopal

Indore

Tapti

Hyderabad

Krishna

11

Bhima

Madras

Pondicherry

Kanpur

Jodhpur

Great Indian

Thar

Chambal

Luni

17

Rann of Kutch

Ahmadabad

4

Gulf of Khambhat

Bombay

Western Ghats

8

Bangalore

Mysore

Salem

9

19

Eastern

Ghats

Jaffna

G. of Mannar

SRI LANKA
[Ceylon]

Colombo

ANDAMAN SEA

G. of Martaban

Rangoon

*Andaman
Islands
[India]*

*Nicobar
Islands
[India]*

BAY

OF

BENGAL

I N D I A N

O C E A N

*Laccadive
Islands*

MALDIVES

ARABIAN

SEA

Tropic of Cancer

Karachi

Indus

Nal

INDIAN STATES

1 ANDHRA PRADESH
2 ASSAM
3 BIHAR
4 GUJARAT
5 HARYANA
6 HIMACHAL PRADESH
7 JAMMU & KASHMIR
8 KARNATAKA
9 KERALA
10 MADHYA PRADESH
11 MAHARASHTRA
12 MANIPUR
13 MEGHALAYA
14 NAGALAND
15 ORISSA
16 PUNJAB
17 RAJASTHAN
18 SIKKIM
19 TAMIL NADU
20 TRIPURA
21 UTTAR PRADESH
22 WEST BENGAL

HEIGHT IN FEET AND METERS		
feet	meters	
18,000	6,000	
12,000	4,000	
6,000	2,000	
3,000	1,000	
1,000	300	
0	0	Above Sea Level
		Sea Level

| 0 | 200 | 400 | miles |
| 0 | 200 | 400 | 600 | 800 | km |

Climate

The most influential feature of the climate is monsoon weather. A monsoon is a wind that blows in one direction part of the year and in the opposite direction during another part of the year. In India, monsoon winds bring months of daily rain, followed by months of daily sunshine each year. Rainy months are usually June through September. In the far south, a second monsoon rain hits from October to December.

January through May each year is dry. But everybody talks about the coming monsoon. Too much or too little rain can hurt crops. Some areas have to store all they can during the annual rain so there will be water for drinking and washing later on. The rainiest place on Earth is Cherrapunji in northeast India. The average annual rainfall is 450 inches (1143 cm) — more than ten times the amount received by Washington, DC. One very rainy year brought 1,042 inches (2,647 cm) of rain to Cherrapunji!

The monsoons can be dangerous when little or no rain falls. In 1943, the state of West Bengal lost 1.5 million people. They starved to death after lack of rain killed the crops. One of the driest deserts on Earth is the Thar in northwest India. Mountains to the east of the desert cause the clouds to drop their rain, leaving nothing but hot winds by the time the clouds reach the desert.

Weather is a major cause of disasters in the country. In 1864, 1942, 1971, and 1977, cyclones and flooding killed thousands around the Bay of Bengal. Temperatures well below zero are common in the Himalayan Mountains near China. Central India in March, April, and May has temperatures during the day as high as 120° F (50° C).

Industry, Agriculture, and Natural Resources

Northeast and southeast India have some of the best farmland on Earth. Rice is grown in both areas, making India second only to China in the amount of rice produced. Tea grows in the far north, where the weather is cooler and damp. In northwestern India, wheat needs less water and grows well. This part of the country is known as India's food bowl. Other important foods are dairy products, fish, mutton, fruit, root crops, seeds for cooking oil, and spices. India is now the fourth largest producer of food on Earth. For 30 years, the country has used modern fertilizer and greatly improved seeds. Most years, there is enough food for everyone.

A crop that is crucial to India's industry is cotton. For centuries, Indians showed the rest of the world how to weave and dye beautiful cloth. The word *chintz* is Hindi and means "spotted cloth." Chintz caused a sensation when it was brought to Europe 300 years ago. Handicrafts are still important, but there are many modern industries as well. They include steelmaking, machine tools, and electronics. The country is a leader in making nuclear energy and has more thorium — a nuclear fuel — than any other country.

Other major raw materials include coal, oil, wood, iron ore, nitrogen, and phosphate for fertilizer, plus aluminum, copper, zinc, and lead. India has the largest railway system in Asia. It builds trains and sells them to many other countries. Indian resources and industry are continuing the production of good highways and modern ocean ships. High above, Indian satellites have successfully orbited the Earth.

Technology has not always been good to India. In 1984, deadly gas escaped from an American-owned pesticide plant in the city of Bhopal. Officially 2,500 people died, but the actual number may be as high as 8,000. More than 20,000 were blinded or otherwise injured. Union-Carbide, the US company, is being sued for $3 billion by the government of India. The money will go to survivors and lawyers.

People

The people of India number over 800,000,000, making it the second most populated country in the world, right behind China. There are probably more different kinds of people in India than anywhere on Earth. Short, tall, light, dark, fat, thin — there is even one group that scientists say are the world's hairiest humans!

India's cities are world famous. But the country's 500,000 villages are where most people live. The average Indian is about 30 years of age, is married, has four or more living children, cannot read, earns a living farming rented land, and lives in a building with two or three rooms. He or she has never been farther than 20 miles (32 km) from home and is a Hindu.

A poor crop can drive this male or female to one of India's already crowded cities. Rural Indians do not see city streets as ways to get from one place to another. They use streets as places to live, sleeping in the open whenever there is no rain. A city like Calcutta, with almost 10 million residents, has 300,000 homeless. They are the poorest people on Earth. Nearly one-third live in poverty, near starvation. Though life expectancy has climbed from age 32 in the 1940s to 55 today, malnutrition and poor living conditions result in a high death rate among the poor.

People of all stations in life respect and follow the ideals set forth by Mahatma Gandhi of humility and self-denial. They also value social harmony, a fact which may help explain their patience.

The family is the center of an Indian's life. In most families, aunts, uncles, and other relatives live together. Parents are treasured and respected, and they are cared for in their old age by younger family members. Traditionally, families were and are still large with at least six children. Modern city families are often smaller with between two and four children.

Language

There are two major families of language in India. One family comes from the language spoken by Aryans who invaded from central Asia 3,500 years ago. The other comes from the Dravidian languages of India's original inhabitants. The language introduced by the Aryans is called Indo-European. That is because the Aryan language is somewhat like a number of European languages.

Today, there are 15 major languages spoken in India. The official language is Hindi, an Aryan tongue. Government workers speak to each other in Hindi and in English, learned from the British. There also is a written language, called Sanscrit, that was once spoken widely but is now used only in Hindu religious books.

Each major language has hundreds of dialects. And there are hundreds of local languages. Once in a while, non-Hindi speaking Indians will protest official use of Hindi. There are 97 versions of Hindi.

Education

Only one Indian in three can read. Because sons are considered more valuable than daughters, they are more often sent to school. So twice as many men can read as women. The number of readers is expected to increase as more and more villages get primary schools (grades 1-5). However, some Indians still keep children out of school to work, and the proportion of the people who can read has not increased in over ten years. The government says schooling is free and required for children between six and fourteen, but there are far too few schools and teachers to make this goal a reality. Poverty and poor health also keep many children from getting an education.

India has many modern universities, but only a small percentage of students attend college. Many Indians go to college in England, the United States, and Canada.

Arts and Crafts

Art is alive in India. It can be a drama that tells of gods and goddesses or a group performing Hindu dances thousands of years old. Or it can be a sitar performance.

During the 1960s young people in the West became familiar with the sound and appearance of the sitar after the Beatles went to India to meditate and learn to play this ancient instrument. In the years that followed, Ravi Shankar, an Indian sitar player, became famous through records and concerts in North America and Europe.

The sitar is a stringed instrument with a long neck. The rounded body is made of a gourd, and another gourd is mounted on the neck. The sitar usually has six or more strings that are plucked and others that simply vibrate with the ones that are plucked. The sitar is played with a *mizrab*, a pick made of wire which is attached to the player's forefinger. Sometimes the player strums the vibrating, or sympathetic, strings with a pinky fingernail that has been allowed to grow very, very long for this purpose. The sitar player sits cross-legged on the floor and rests the body of the sitar on his or her left foot.

Crafts are thousands of years old, too. But they are kept alive because they remain popular in India and elsewhere. Pottery can take the form of a painted vase, a Hindu god, or an almost lifesize animal. Weavers create ancient designs on rugs and cloth using hand looms. Jewelers make gold and silver rings and bracelets that cause Indian women to jangle when they walk. Because children usually do the same jobs as parents, these skills are passed from one generation to the next.

Arts and crafts usually have religious ties. That's especially true in buildings where sacred themes are carried out. Dozens of mosques and temples across India are world famous for their magnificent architecture and religious art.

Sports and Recreation

Sports and games introduced by the British are popular in India. Polo, which the British discovered in Pakistan, is played by wealthy Indians. So is cricket, a game similar to baseball. Soccer is a popular sport, as are swimming, sailing, fishing, hiking, and wrestling. In large cities, roaming entertainers do magic tricks, tell fortunes, charm snakes, perform gymnastics, and entertain in other ways.

A hugely popular form of relaxation is the movies. The Indian film industry is the world's largest, producing more movies than that of any other country. Each year, more than 700 features are made. They are often tales of India's past or romance films filled with singing and dancing. Recent movies showing the role of women or problems in modern society have been popular. Most movies are in the official Hindi language. Even medium-sized cities have over 100 movie theaters.

New Delhi

India's capital, known as both Delhi and New Delhi, has been a city since at least 1000 BC. Today on the banks of the Yamuna River, ruins still stand to testify to the skill of India's ancient builders. Forts and palaces, shrines and gateways were built by dynasty after dynasty. Each ruler tried to leave Delhi more splendid than he found it, and many succeeded.

Delhi today is two cities, with a combined population of over five million people. It is situated in the north-central union territory of Delhi on the west bank of the Yamuna River.

Old Delhi is Shahjahanabad, a city built in the 17th century. It is a maze of winding streets, alleys, and markets. Everywhere you go in Old Delhi, you can see the sandstone ramparts of the Purana Qila, known as the Old Fort or the Red Fort. At the heart of the city is the Jama Masjid Mosque with its marble domes.

In Old Delhi visitors can almost imagine themselves in the India of the Moghuls. The filigreed ivory and gold embroidered silks evoke an earlier time. You can walk through the streets lined with silversmiths and jewelers and bargain for tiny bottles of strong oriental perfumes.

New Delhi is another story. This is the heart of modern India, the seat of the government, and the center of the city that Delhi is today. The main architecture of the city was designed by British architect Edward Lutyens at the height of Britain's dominance of India.

Delhi is an important industrial center as well as a tourist and government center. Its products include textiles, chemicals, metal products, rubber goods, machine tools, and electronic components.

New Delhi Republic Day Parade.

Indians in North America

Between twenty and thirty thousand Indians migrate to the United States each year. Many are students who came to US colleges and universities and wanted to stay. Those who apply for citizenship are often professionals — physicians, engineers, scientists, and others whose skills would be in demand in either country. Most of the thousands of students eventually return to India.

Small Indian communities exist in New York City, Toronto, Vancouver, and Los Angeles. Their communities are not always distinct like those of other immigrant groups who tend to live together in one area when they come to a new country. Indians in North America often have a centralized business district, but they do not live in any one part of the city.

More Books About India

Here are some more books about India. If you are interested in them, check your library. They may be helpful in doing research for the "Things to Do" projects that follow.

India: An Ancient Land, A New Nation. Sarin (Dillon)
Mahatma Gandhi. Nicholson (Gareth Stevens)

Mother Teresa. Gray (Gareth Stevens)
Seasons of Splendor: Tales, Myths and Legends from India.
   Jaffrey (Macmillan)
Take a Trip to India. Lye (Franklin Watts)
We Live in India. Sandal (Franklin Watts)

Glossary of Useful Indian Terms

caste (cast) . . . . one of four groups that a person can be born into. Originally the castes determined what work a person would do.

daal (dahl) . . . . a lentil dish, like a thick soup.

Mahatma (mah-HAHT-mah) . . . . a Sanskrit word that means "Great Soul." The title is given to men of great wisdom, such as Gandhi.

masaala (mah-SAHL-a) . . . . a blend of spices made by each family to flavor food.

namaste (nah-MAH-stee) . . . . a gesture of greeting or good-bye. A person bends gently with palms together below the chin.

puja (POO-jah) . . . . a prayer service.

satyagraha (sah-tee-ah-GRAH-hah) . . . Gandhi's policy of non-violent resistance to injustice.

Things to Do — Research Projects

Something is always happening in India. Sometimes the news is of weather, which can affect the food supply of millions. Other times it is about India's disputes with its neighbors, or its complicated and challenging politics or its technological advances. As you read about India, or any country, keep in mind the importance of current facts. Some of the research projects that follow need accurate, up-to-date information. That is why current newspapers and magazines are useful sources of information. Two publications your library may have will tell you about recent magazine and newspaper articles on many topics:

The Reader's Guide to Periodical Literature
Children's Magazine Guide

For accurate answers to questions about such topics of current interest as India's border wars, look up *India* in one of these publications. They will lead you to the most up-to-date information you can find.

1. Mohandas K. Gandhi was the greatest spiritual leader of our century. See what you can find out about political and social movements that you believe in that have been affected by his teachings.

2. How far is Jodhpur from where you live? Using maps, travel guides, travel agents, or any other resources you know of, find out how you could get there and how long it would take.

3. India is the birthplace of some of the world's largest and oldest religions. Others have found in India a place to worship as they please. Find out more about the beliefs of one of these religions: Hinduism, Buddhism, Sikhism, Jainism, or Islam. In what ways do you share the beliefs and values of its followers?

More Things to Do — Activities

These projects are designed to encourage you to think more about India. They offer ideas for interesting group or individual projects for school or home.

1. India is a land of many festivals. With a group of friends or classmates, investigate further. Plan an Indian festival. Be sure everyone understands the history and importance of the festival as well as the fun and food.

2. Many of the children of the world go to bed hungry and sick. Many of these children are in India. Find an organization that provides food and medical care for children in India or somewhere else and see what you can do to help.

3. Think of a job or career you would like. Would you be able to do this work in India? Would being male or female make a difference? Would your ethnic or religious background make a difference?

4. If you would like a pen pal in India, write to these people:

> International Pen Friends
> P.O. Box 290065
> Brooklyn, New York 11229-0001

Be sure to tell them what country you want your pen pal to be from. Also, include your full name, address, and age.

Index